D1606929

LOOKING INSIDE

EARTH

BY MARTHA LONDON

Published by The Child's World®
1980 Lookout Drive • Mankato, MN 56003-1705
800-599-READ • www.childsworld.com

Photographs ©: Shutterstock Images, cover, 1, 2; iStockphoto, 5, 13, 14, 16, 21, 24; Mario Guti/iStockphoto, 6; Lindsay Lou/iStockphoto, 8; Jef Folkerts/iStockphoto, 9; Justin Reznick/iStockphoto, 11; SDO/NASA, 17; Vadim Sadovski/Shutterstock Images, 19

ISBN 9781503835184
LCCN 2019943113

Printed in the United States of America

ABOUT THE AUTHOR
Martha London writes books for young readers full-time. When she isn't writing, you can find her hiking in the woods.

TABLE OF CONTENTS

CHAPTER ONE

Earth Has Layers

Earth is made of layers. Scientists divide Earth into four parts. The crust is the top layer. Under the crust are the mantle, outer core, and inner core. Each layer has different features. Some of the layers are solid. Others are liquid.

The **radius** of Earth is nearly 4,000 miles (6,440 km). Within Earth, temperatures can reach more than 10,000 degrees Fahrenheit (5,540°C). Scientists cannot reach any layer below the crust. The temperature is too high, and the layers are too deep. To learn about Earth's layers, scientists use tools that measure earthquakes. Earthquakes cause waves of energy that move underground. Earthquake waves look different as they pass through different types of rock. Scientists study the waves to learn about Earth's layers.

Layers of Earth

Inner Core

Outer Core

Mantle

Crust

The crust contains all life on Earth.

CHAPTER TWO

The Crust

The crust is like Earth's shell. Scientists know more about the crust than they do about Earth's other layers. The crust is the thinnest layer. It is just 1 percent of Earth, but it supports all life on Earth. The crust is made of solid rock. It has different kinds of rocks. Some rocks are made of many tiny bits of rock. Some form under heat and pressure. Others come from volcanoes. They form when lava cools. Most rocks in the crust formed this way. Some parts of the crust are thicker than others. The thickness depends on the type of crust.

People can dive between two tectonic plates at Silfra in Iceland.

Earth has two different types of crust. They are oceanic crust and continental crust. Oceanic crust lies under oceans. It is **denser** than continental crust. Heavy oceanic crust sinks below the lighter continental crust. It melts in the mantle below.

Continental crust makes up continents. It is thicker than oceanic crust. It is also older. Unlike oceanic crust, continental crust is less likely to sink and melt. This means that it lasts longer. The oldest rocks in continental crust are around 4 billion years old. The oldest rocks in oceanic crust are only about 200 million years old.

Earth's crust is made of sections called **tectonic plates**. Tectonic plates are constantly moving over the mantle. As the plates move, sometimes they get stuck. When they finally shift, the force shakes the area around them. This is what causes earthquakes.

Creating Mountains

Mountains are part of Earth's crust. They take millions of years to form. Tectonic plates and volcanoes both create mountains. Sometimes one plate rises higher than another. Other times, plates collide. When they crash together, the two plates slowly push up. When volcanoes erupt, lava flows out and cools. Over time, layers of lava build up into mountains.

CHAPTER THREE

The Mantle

The mantle sits below the crust. It is the thickest layer. The crust is only about 30 miles (50 km) thick. By contrast, the mantle is 1,800 miles (2,900 km) thick. That is the about distance from New York City to Orlando, Florida, and back again. The mantle makes up 84 percent of Earth.

Like Earth's crust, the mantle is made of rock. It is mostly solid. But some of the mantle is **molten**. Scientists compare the mantle to soft plastic. It can shift and move around. The mantle is very hot. It is more than 1,000 degrees Fahrenheit (540°C) near the crust. At the bottom of the mantle, temperatures triple. These high temperatures allow the mantle to flow.

Lava is molten rock that has reached Earth's surface. When molten rock is under the surface, it is called magma.

11

Sections of Earth's crust sink into the mantle over time. As they sink, they soften and melt. Hotter material rises to the top of the mantle. Cooler material sinks. This movement is called **convection**. Convection is always happening in the mantle.

Sometimes molten rock reaches Earth's surface. Lava flows out of cracks in the crust. The lava from volcanoes hardens into new crust. Often this new crust is formed on the ocean floor. The crust is thinnest there, and lava can easily break through.

CONVECTION

Convection in the mantle is very slow. It flows at rates of only a few centimeters per year.

Early Earth's surface was an ocean of molten rock.

CHAPTER FOUR

The Outer Core

Below the mantle is the outer core. The outer core is about 1,370 miles (2,200 km) thick. Liquid metal makes up the outer core. It is 80 percent iron. The other 20 percent is a mixture of nickel and other **elements**. When Earth was still new about 4.5 billion years ago, it was a molten planet. Heat and pressure caused heavy elements such as iron to sink toward the center. The iron settled in Earth's core.

The outer core is very hot. Its temperatures range from 8,130 to 9,930 degrees Fahrenheit (4,500 to 5,500°C). The outer core's metals are constantly heating and cooling. As a result, they rotate through the outer core. This is another case of convection.

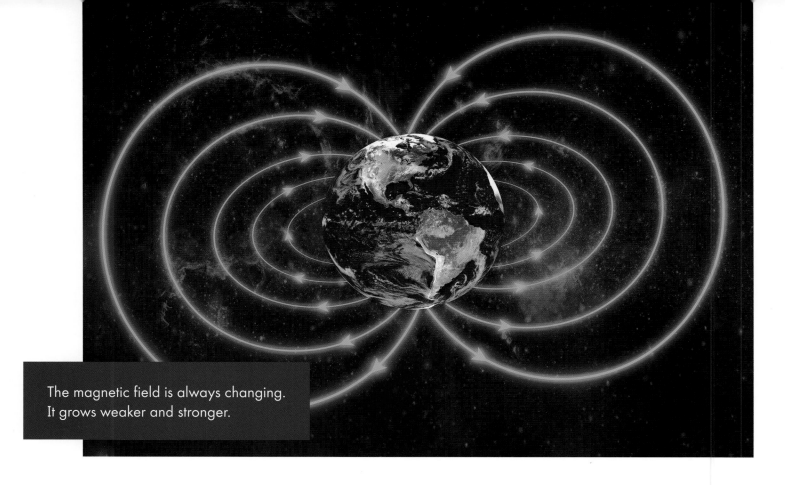

The magnetic field is always changing. It grows weaker and stronger.

The convection in the outer core helps create Earth's **magnetic field**. A magnetic field is an invisible area that has a magnetic force. Magnetic fields come from moving electricity. The movement of liquid metal in the core produces electric **currents**. As Earth spins, these currents create the magnetic field. The field surrounds the planet. It stretches far into space.

The magnetic field acts as a shield against solar winds. Solar winds are caused by explosions on the sun. Matter from the sun blasts toward Earth. It can harm living things. But the magnetic field protects Earth from most of the harmful effects of solar winds. Without the magnetic field, solar winds would destroy the **atmosphere** over time.

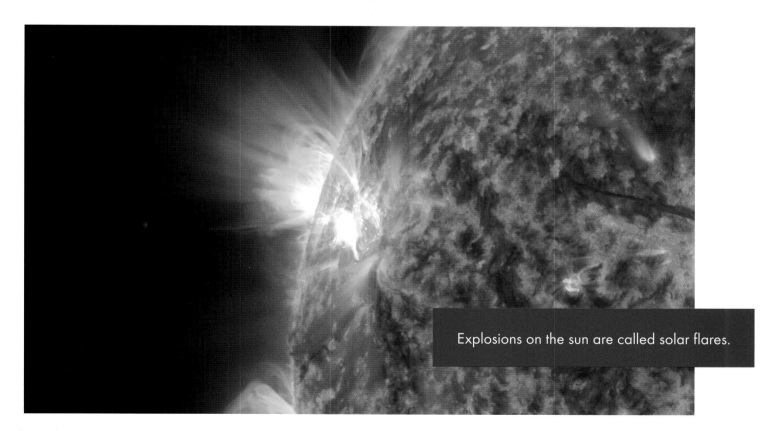

Explosions on the sun are called solar flares.

CHAPTER FIVE

The Inner Core

Earth's inner core is a solid ball. The inner core is about 9,390 degrees Fahrenheit (5,200°C). This would be hot enough to melt the metals in the core. But the inner core is under a lot of pressure. The weight of the planet presses on the inner core. This pressure turns the metals to a solid. When the metals turn to a solid, they release heat. The boundary between the outer and inner core is about 10,800 degrees Fahrenheit (5,980°C). That is as hot as the surface of the sun.

The inner core has a radius of 760 miles (1,220 km). That means the inner core is just slightly smaller than the moon. The inner core is slowly growing. As parts of the outer core sink toward the inner core, they become solid. This process takes billions of years. Scientists think it would take about 91 billion years for the entire core to become completely solid.

The inner core spins almost 1 second faster than the rest of Earth.

Scientists believe the inner core is much younger than the rest of the planet. Earth did not always have a solid inner core. It was once all liquid. During this time, the magnetic field around Earth was very weak. Dangerous solar winds from the sun passed through the field. They harmed the planet. But about 565 million years ago, the solid core began to form. When the inner core became solid, it strengthened the magnetic field. Life could then flourish. All of Earth's layers help support the planet and the life that lives on it.

FAST FACTS

- Earth has four layers: the crust, mantle, outer core, and inner core.

- The crust is the thinnest layer.

- The crust supports all life on Earth.

- The mantle is the thickest layer.

- Convection is the sinking of cooling material and the rising of hot material.

- The boundary between the outer and inner core is as hot as the surface of the sun.

- The outer core creates a magnetic field that protects Earth.

- The inner core is solid. The solid inner core strengthens the magnetic field.

- The inner core is about the size of the moon.

GLOSSARY

atmosphere (AT-muss-fihr) The atmosphere is a ball of air that surrounds Earth. Solar winds can harm the atmosphere.

convection (kun-VEK-shun) Convection is the movement of heat through liquid. Convection happens in the mantle.

currents (KUR-uhnts) Currents are the flow of something. Electricity flows in currents.

denser (DEN-sur) Denser means heavier or more packed together. Oceanic crust is denser than continental crust.

elements (EL-uh-muhnts) Elements are matter that cannot be broken down into anything else. Heavy elements sink to the center of the core.

magnetic field (mag-NEH-tik FEELD) A magnetic field is the magnetic force that surrounds something. The magnetic field protects Earth from solar winds.

molten (MOHLT-un) Molten means melted by heat. Lava is molten rock.

radius (RAY-dee-uss) The radius is the distance between the center and outer edge of a ball or circle. Earth's radius is nearly 4,000 miles (6,440 km).

tectonic plates (tek-TON-ik PLAYTS) Tectonic plates are large sections of Earth's crust. Tectonic plates move over the mantle.

TO LEARN MORE

IN THE LIBRARY

Ganeri, Anita. *Eruption!: The Story of Volcanoes*. New York, NY: DK Publishing, 2015.

Goldstein, Margaret J. *Discover Earth*. Minneapolis, MN: Lerner, 2018.

London, Martha. *The Rock Cycle*. Mankato, MN: The Child's World, 2019.

ON THE WEB

Visit our website for links about Earth:

childsworld.com/links

Note to Parents, Teachers, and Librarians: We routinely verify our Web links to make sure they are safe and active sites. So encourage your readers to check them out!

INDEX